BirdNote

JOURNAL

A Birdwatcher's Companion from
the Popular Public Radio Show

Illustrations by
EMILY POOLE

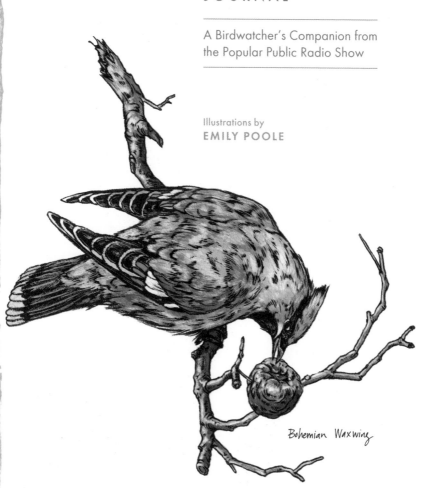

Bohemian Waxwing

SASQUATCH BOOKS
SEATTLE

Varied Thrush

Contents

Northern Cardinal

About *BirdNote*

BirdNote began in 2004 as a project under the auspices of Seattle Audubon. *BirdNote* founder Chris Peterson, then executive director of Seattle Audubon, gathered a team of writers to craft compelling stories about the intriguing ways of birds. Ornithological advisers ensured scientific accuracy. A professional narrator and sound engineer gave voice to the stories. And dedicated staff, volunteers, and contractors helped form the final product. With generous support from benefactors, *BirdNote* was launched on air in February 2005 by KPLU-FM (now KNKX) of Seattle-Tacoma. In 2006 *BirdNote* was incorporated as an independent nonprofit under the name Tune In to Nature. Since then *BirdNote* has produced more than 1,500 shows and podcasts, as well as several videos.

The mission of *BirdNote* is to tell stories that connect listeners with the joy and wonder of nature. By sharing vivid, sound-rich stories about birds and the challenges they face, *BirdNote* inspires listeners to care about the natural world—and take steps to protect it.

The two-minute stories can be heard on air, online, and via podcast. Shows reach an estimated audience of more than two million people in four hundred communities across the United States, as well as in Canada and the Philippines. Select episodes are also available via the Public Radio Exchange (PRX.org) and embedded in *Living on Earth*, distributed by Public Radio International. The stories feature the sounds of hundreds of species of birds, most from the vast audio collection of the Macaulay Library at the Cornell Lab of Ornithology, and are told by Mary McCann, Michael Stein, and occasional guest hosts.

As an independent media producer, *BirdNote* is grateful for the airtime provided by public radio stations and for the financial support from individual donors, foundations, and corporate underwriters that make all its work possible.

The stories in this journal are derived from ones originally heard on the *BirdNote* radio show, written by lead writer Bob Sundstrom along with Ellen Blackstone, Chris Peterson, Todd Peterson, Adam Sedgley, and Frances Wood. For more information about *BirdNote* and on the birds featured in its stories, visit BirdNote.org.

We hope you will make this journal your own. Whether you travel far and wide to see birds or watch the ones right in your back yard, you can make notes and sketches in your own words and in your own way. Following birds through the year is an interesting path to understanding their life cycle and their needs. Keeping track of when the first migratory bird arrives in spring will attune you to changes in seasons. Your life list can be a simple list of birds, or you can include notes and observations. We hope you enjoy using this journal and that it brings you closer to birds and nature.

Sanderling

FIELD NOTES

PLACE / DATE Sept Oct 2020
BIRD Pine Siskin
NOTES Fichie saw at gold finch feeder

PLACE / DATE
BIRD American Goldfinch
NOTES NYGER+ SuN flower hearts feeder

PLACE / DATE Summer in O.B, on Boat
BIRD Double Breasted Cormorant
NOTES

PLACE / DATE
BIRD Downy Woodpecker
NOTES
    at SUET feeder

In September I started shopping
at bird food Store deffrent
types of food + feeders

3/21 humming bird feeder start 3/29/21

PLACE / DATE

BIRD Hairy Woodpecker

NOTES at SUET feeder

PLACE / DATE

BIRD ~~Flicker~~

NOTES ~~Suet feeder~~

PLACE / DATE

BIRD Black capped chickadee

NOTES

PLACE / DATE

BIRD Tufted titmouse

NOTES Sag Harbor

PLACE / DATE

BIRD House Wren

NOTES

PLACE / DATE

BIRD Northern Mockingbird

NOTES

PLACE / DATE

BIRD Starling

NOTES

PLACE / DATE

BIRD Sparrow house, tree

NOTES

PLACE / DATE

BIRD *Dark eyed Junco*

NOTES

PLACE / DATE

BIRD *Northern Cardinal*

NOTES

PLACE / DATE

BIRD *Red Winged Black Bird*

NOTES

Jones Beach drive

PLACE / DATE 3/28/21   yard

BIRD *Brown Headed Cowbird* 1

NOTES

Gathering Clues from a Bird's Behavior

You've spotted an unfamiliar bird. How do you figure out what it is? Apart from color and size, what do you look for?

A bird's behavior offers many clues. You'll see flycatchers "fly-catch," darting out to catch a bug in the air. And woodpeckers peck, whether foraging for tidbits under the bark or carving out a nest cavity.

To distinguish one bird from a similar one, watch what the bird does. Does it flick its wings? Bob up and down? Flip its tail? A field guide usually mentions these behaviors and can help you determine which bird is which.

Is the bird feeding on the ground or high in a tree? *Peterson Field Guide to Birds of North America* says the Eastern Towhee "rummages among leaf litter," while the Olive-sided Flycatcher "perches on dead snags at tops of trees."

How does it move? According to *Peterson*, the Horned Lark "walks, does not hop," and an American Robin makes "short runs, then pauses."

Does a bird work its way up a tree, or down? The Brown Creeper, a drab little bird that blends in with the bark, works its way up a tree. When it's done with one tree, it flies back to the bottom of the next. Nuthatches work their way *down* a tree, finding morsels that most creepers and most woodpeckers would miss.

Watching birds is a bit like detective work. Gather enough clues, and you'll solve the mystery.

Olive - sided Flycatcher

PLACE / DATE

BIRD house finch

NOTES

PLACE / DATE

BIRD Canada Goose

NOTES all over

PLACE / DATE

BIRD Wood duck

NOTES Hoyt farm

PLACE / DATE

BIRD Mallard

NOTES

PLACE / DATE

BIRD Phesant

NOTES Pa woods

PLACE / DATE

BIRD Wild Turkey

NOTES Pa woods

PLACE / DATE

BIRD Cormorant

NOTES Boat

PLACE / DATE

BIRD Blue Heron

NOTES Boat

PLACE / DATE

BIRD *Great Egret*

NOTES *Boat*

PLACE / DATE

BIRD *Osprey*

NOTES *Boat*

PLACE / DATE

BIRD *Bald Eagle*

NOTES *Florida*

PLACE / DATE

BIRD *Red tailed Hawk*

NOTES *Parkway*

PLACE / DATE

BIRD Gull

NOTES Wantagh Park

PLACE / DATE

BIRD Pigeon Rock

NOTES

PLACE / DATE

BIRD Morning Dove

NOTES Backyard

PLACE / DATE

BIRD Owls 4 different type

NOTES farm on LI

PLACE / DATE

BIRD Humming Birds

NOTES California

PLACE / DATE

BIRD falcon

NOTES NY City

PLACE / DATE

BIRD Blue Jay

NOTES

PLACE / DATE

BIRD Crow

NOTES

Night Voices

Think a birder's day is over when the sun goes down? Think again . . .

At the close of a summer day, most songbirds go silent. The final notes of a thrush—be it a Veery, a Swainson's, a Hermit, or an American Robin—reverberate in near darkness.

And as if on cue, the true birds of the night now make their voices known. Let's go on an owl prowl . . .

In an eastern woodland, the eerie trills and whinnies of an Eastern Screech-Owl are among the first sounds of the night. Mates trill to one another during courtship and whinny to defend territory.

Meanwhile, as night falls west of the Rockies, a different pair of small owls combines voices, hooting a rhythmic duet. These night singers, Western Screech-Owls, make their home in low-elevation woodlands and deserts.

But there's another bird whose voice will drown out the loudest of screech-owls: the Barred Owl, a large, stocky bird of forests, swamps, and suburban parks. "Who cooks for you? Who cooks for you all?" it hoots. Pairs may break into a rollicking duet, known as the "monkey call."

Whether you're owl-prowling deep in a forest, in open country, or in a city park, you might spot a Great Horned Owl. Listen for the call birders describe as "Who's awake? Me too."

Owls aren't the only ones out and about during the night. A strange family of birds known as "nightjars" also inhabits that parallel universe. Many seem to say their own names, and depending on where you are in the country, you might hear "poor-will, poor-will, poor-will," or "whip-poor-will, whip-poor-will," or "Chuck-will's-widow, Chuck-will's-widow."

Listen, too, for a Killdeer, a type of shorebird, as it wings its way through the night, crying plaintively, "killDEER, killDEER, killDEER."

Even some songbirds, known mostly for their day songs, can be heard proclaiming their territories at night. The Northern Mockingbird, actually a bird of the American South, imitates more than a dozen birds, all through the day and right into the night. And the Yellow-breasted Chat, the largest warbler in the United States, also sings at night.

All in all, great reasons not to end your birding day when the sun goes down!

Barred Owl
Feather

PLACE / DATE
BIRD Robin
NOTES

PLACE / DATE
BIRD ~~Grackt~~ GRACKLE
NOTES

PLACE / DATE yard, 11/20/20
BIRD Chimney SWIFT 1
NOTES
under feeder 8AM few other Birds

PLACE / DATE Back yard
BIRD
NOTES 6 feeders 37 perches
5 different food types
lots of cool Birds

PLACE / DATE yard 12-4-20

BIRD female Harry Woodpecker

NOTES

PLACE / DATE yard 12-19-20

BIRD Phoebe

NOTES pair

COOPERS?

PLACE / DATE HAWK 12/28/20

BIRD

NOTES he got + ate a Blue Jay

PLACE / DATE yard 3/29/21

BIRD Savanah Sparrow

NOTES

PLACE / DATE Backyard 4/24/21
BIRD Boat tailed Grackle
NOTES

PLACE / DATE Wantagh Park
BIRD Laughing Gull
NOTES

PLACE / DATE O B Boat
BIRD Great Skua
NOTES

PLACE / DATE Carolina N. 3/21
BIRD Bald Eagle
NOTES By todds row track

PLACE / DATE

BIRD

NOTES

PLACE / DATE

BIRD

NOTES

PLACE / DATE

BIRD

NOTES

PLACE / DATE

BIRD

NOTES

PLACE / DATE

BIRD

NOTES

PLACE / DATE

BIRD

NOTES

PLACE / DATE

BIRD

NOTES

PLACE / DATE

BIRD

NOTES

Gardening with Birds in Mind

Native plants sustain native birds. Whether birds and plants evolved together or birds learned to relish the plants, the combination works.

It's no accident that Rufous Hummingbirds arrive in the Northwest in spring, tired and thirsty, just as the red-flowering currant blooms. And Swainson's Thrushes seem to time their migration to the fruiting of shrubs. Rose-breasted Grosbeaks depend primarily on fruit during their fall migration, and native elderberries and serviceberries are ready just in time.

Native plants offer sustenance year-round: nectar in spring and summer, along with berries and fruits, nuts, and seeds in autumn and winter. They provide cover: shelter from the weather and protection from predators. They also tend to support native insects, which are an important food source for birds. Native plants provide natural, sustainable habitat that welcomes native birds to your yard.

And in winter? Some of the best ways to help backyard birds through the cold season may mean doing less, not more.

First, leave the leaves. Tasty insects and spiders live underneath. Backyard birds like the towhee and the Song Sparrow will pick and kick through leaves again and again. Leave the leaves where they've drifted or rake them up under your plantings.

Second, don't deadhead the plants in your garden. Birds such as Pine Siskins, House Finches, and goldfinches will snack on dead flower heads all winter long.

Third, build an insect hotel. Okay, there's some work involved in this one. But it's a cool project for kids and adults to do together. Make a structure out of natural objects and "found" items, such as rotten logs, reeds, bamboo, and bundles of twigs or leaves, to create little hidey-holes for insects. It's also a great way to repurpose old bricks and flowerpots and bits of wood stacked together in your own sculpture. Some of the cozy hotel guests will become food for wrens and other birds. Even a simple brush pile offers a bounty of insects and a bit of cover from a storm.

So park the rake in the shed and the clippers too. And skip the herbicides and pesticides. The birds will thank you.

Northern Cardinal Feather

PLACE / DATE

BIRD

NOTES

PLACE / DATE

BIRD

NOTES

PLACE / DATE

BIRD

NOTES

PLACE / DATE

BIRD

NOTES

PLACE / DATE

BIRD

NOTES

PLACE / DATE

BIRD

NOTES

PLACE / DATE

BIRD

NOTES

PLACE / DATE

BIRD

NOTES

PLACE / DATE

BIRD

NOTES

PLACE / DATE

BIRD

NOTES

PLACE / DATE

BIRD

NOTES

PLACE / DATE

BIRD

NOTES

PLACE / DATE

BIRD

NOTES

PLACE / DATE

BIRD

NOTES

PLACE / DATE

BIRD

NOTES

PLACE / DATE

BIRD

NOTES

PLACE / DATE

BIRD

NOTES

PLACE / DATE

BIRD

NOTES

PLACE / DATE

BIRD

NOTES

PLACE / DATE

BIRD

NOTES

Planning a Birding Trip

One of the great joys of birding—or birdwatching—is that birds are nearly everywhere in the world.

Have a free day on your business trip or a spare morning on your family vacation? A birding trail may be your best bet. More than forty states have published at least one birding trail map, so you're likely to find one to suit your needs. Most maps contain multiple loops that were selected by the local bird experts to cover a variety of habitats and the avian specialties of the area. Maps generally include notes about accessibility for the mobility impaired.

If you are looking for a particular species, search Cornell's eBird—a website where birders submit their sightings. You can also join a mailing list for a specific area and ask for advice from the members. (You'll find such lists on the American Birding Association website, ABA.org.) If you join a list for the area where you live—or where you intend to travel—you'll be alerted when unusual birds are being seen.

There are many tour groups that cater to birders. Ecotourism—hiring a local guide when you visit an exotic destination—can be a win-win-win situation. You receive the services of a local expert. The guide has employment. And the birds thrive because those communities have an economic incentive to protect the birds and their habitats. Wherever you go, let the locals know why you're there: for the birds!

No matter how much research you do, nothing can match the eyes and ears of a local expert. If you are traveling in the United

States, consider getting in touch with the local Audubon chapter to see if they offer field trips. An easy way to find plenty of local experts—as well as a great place to go birding—is to attend a birding festival. No matter the month, state, or bird of interest, from the Kachemak Bay Shorebird Festival in Homer, Alaska, to "Ding" Darling Days on Sanibel Island on the Gulf Coast of Florida, there's a festival for you. When you go, be sure to wear your binoculars into local businesses—it underscores the economic importance of these festivals.

Public lands offer great opportunities to see birds and other wildlife. National parks and wildlife refuges have birding checklists, and many offer programs and walks for visitors.

Now, just don't forget your binoculars!

Mallard Feather

PLACE / DATE

BIRD

NOTES

PLACE / DATE

BIRD

NOTES

PLACE / DATE

BIRD

NOTES

PLACE / DATE

BIRD

NOTES

PLACE / DATE

BIRD

NOTES

PLACE / DATE

BIRD

NOTES

PLACE / DATE

BIRD

NOTES

PLACE / DATE

BIRD

NOTES

PLACE / DATE

BIRD

NOTES

PLACE / DATE

BIRD

NOTES

PLACE / DATE

BIRD

NOTES

PLACE / DATE

BIRD

NOTES

PLACE / DATE

BIRD

NOTES

PLACE / DATE

BIRD

NOTES

PLACE / DATE

BIRD

NOTES

PLACE / DATE

BIRD

NOTES

PLACE / DATE

BIRD

NOTES

PLACE / DATE

BIRD

NOTES

PLACE / DATE

BIRD

NOTES

PLACE / DATE

BIRD

NOTES

Feed the Birds—Bring Them Up Close

Considering a banquet for your backyard birds? Like any good dinner party, planning is a must.

Birds are fussy. They'll simply toss any seed they don't like—what a waste! This bird wants cracked corn, and another wants millet. You can attract specific birds—and minimize waste—by choosing the right food and the right feeder. Pine Siskins and goldfinches battle over Nyjer thistle. Chickadees thrive on black oil sunflower seeds. Check online birdfeeding stores or retail outlets for the perfect feeder for each type of seed and each type of bird.

Putting out a feeder is easy enough. But the next step is the most important part—keeping it clean and free of disease. A clean feeder is a life-and-death matter to some birds. Pine Siskins, in particular, are prone to salmonellosis, a deadly bacterial disease easily transmitted from bird to bird. For this reason, a thistle feeder shouldn't have a tray.

Clean your feeder at least once a week or more often if you have lots of birds. Throw away stale or moldy seed. You may want to have an extra feeder for each type of seed—one feeds the birds, while the other is being cleaned and dried.

It's especially important to take time to rake up and dispose of the debris under the feeder every few days. It helps prevent disease and discourages visits by four-legged critters.

Oh, and don't forget the woodpeckers! Put out a suet feeder, and watch for nuthatches, jays, wrens, and woodpeckers to join the party!

Downy Woodpecker

PLACE / DATE

BIRD

NOTES

PLACE / DATE

BIRD

NOTES

PLACE / DATE

BIRD

NOTES

PLACE / DATE

BIRD

NOTES

PLACE / DATE

BIRD

NOTES

PLACE / DATE

BIRD

NOTES

PLACE / DATE

BIRD

NOTES

PLACE / DATE

BIRD

NOTES

PLACE / DATE

BIRD

NOTES

PLACE / DATE

BIRD

NOTES

PLACE / DATE

BIRD

NOTES

PLACE / DATE

BIRD

NOTES

PLACE / DATE

BIRD

NOTES

PLACE / DATE

BIRD

NOTES

PLACE / DATE

BIRD

NOTES

PLACE / DATE

BIRD

NOTES

PLACE / DATE

BIRD

NOTES

PLACE / DATE

BIRD

NOTES

PLACE / DATE

BIRD

NOTES

PLACE / DATE

BIRD

NOTES

Become an Avian Landlord—
The Perfect Nestbox

A wren, a chickadee, a titmouse, maybe even a nuthatch . . . one of these small songbirds might make its home in your yard, if you put up the right kind of birdhouse. They're all "cavity nesters," birds that need a hole in a tree—or a birdhouse that serves the same purpose—for nesting. And cavities seem to be at a premium these days.

Look for a nestbox that's plain wood (or make one). None of that fancy stuff—birds prefer their nest sites to be inconspicuous. If the nestbox comes with a cute little dowel perch, remove it. The nesting birds don't need the perch. And the perch just makes it easier for a predator bird to land and go after the eggs or young. Chickadees, especially, might welcome a few fresh wood chips in the bottom of the box.

Here's the important part: grab a ruler and measure the entrance hole. It should be 1⅛ inches. If the entrance hole is too big, use an adapter to reduce the size. That size will let native birds in and keep non-natives out.

Now hang the box where it's out of reach of any predator. Add a baffle or other deterrent if necessary, to keep unwanted guests from reaching the nestbox.

Tree Swallows and bluebirds, both Eastern and Western, also take to nestboxes, but perhaps not right in your yard.

Every autumn, when the nesting season is over and the young have all fledged, clean out the nestbox thoroughly. Soap, water, sunshine, and elbow grease all work. Then either tuck the nestbox away in a dry place for the winter, or hang it back out in case one of your summer residents might decide to make it a winter roost.

In late February or early March, put the clean nestbox out again. The locals are already scouting for cavities, and the swallows and bluebirds will be back before you know it!

PLACE / DATE

BIRD

NOTES

PLACE / DATE

BIRD

NOTES

PLACE / DATE

BIRD

NOTES

PLACE / DATE

BIRD

NOTES

PLACE / DATE

BIRD

NOTES

PLACE / DATE

BIRD

NOTES

PLACE / DATE

BIRD

NOTES

PLACE / DATE

BIRD

NOTES

PLACE / DATE

BIRD

NOTES

PLACE / DATE

BIRD

NOTES

PLACE / DATE

BIRD

NOTES

PLACE / DATE

BIRD

NOTES

PLACE / DATE

BIRD

NOTES

PLACE / DATE

BIRD

NOTES

PLACE / DATE

BIRD

NOTES

PLACE / DATE

BIRD

NOTES

PLACE / DATE

BIRD

NOTES

PLACE / DATE

BIRD

NOTES

PLACE / DATE

BIRD

NOTES

PLACE / DATE

BIRD

NOTES

Birds Need Water, Summer and Winter

Whether it's twenty-seven degrees outside or ninety-seven, birds need water.

It's freezing, and an American Robin is rolling and flopping in the birdbath, flinging water every which way. What on earth is it thinking? Isn't it going to freeze to death with all that water on its feathers? Well, it turns out that bathing in winter actually helps birds' feathers protect them from the cold. The bath washes away particles of dirt that might otherwise prevent the feathers from their waterproofing work. And it probably also helps remove parasites.

Birds need water in all seasons, for drinking and for bathing.

Some things to keep in mind in winter: It will help to put the birdbath on the south side of the house, or in the spot that gets the most sun, or against a sheltered wall. Place it no more than six feet from a tree or shrub, so the birds can fly to cover if a predator comes along. When the water is frozen, you can thaw it with hot water. Or go the slightly more expensive but easier route by adding a heater.

The summer season is generally the driest of the year. Creeks run low or underground. Rain is scarce and temporary puddles gone. Summer is a crucial time to supply your backyard birds with water. Birdbaths set at different heights serve a great variety of birds. Some shy birds come readily to a birdbath set flat on the ground but will rarely visit a birdbath on a pedestal. Leave those for the bolder bathers. Water depth is important too. Many birds prefer shallow water rather than deep. An inch of water—or even less—is ideal for small birds. A wide, shallow birdbath that deepens a bit in the center will suit a broad range of birds. A fine dripper or a mister on a birdbath is also a superb idea. Not only will it keep the bath full with little effort, but small birds, including hummingbirds, often relish a refreshing shower. Many birds find the "drip, drip, drip" of water inviting.

Nothing will bring wondrous songbirds to your yard faster than a ready supply of water.

Ruby-Throated
Hummingbird Feather

PLACE / DATE

BIRD

NOTES

PLACE / DATE

BIRD

NOTES

PLACE / DATE

BIRD

NOTES

PLACE / DATE

BIRD

NOTES

PLACE / DATE

BIRD

NOTES

PLACE / DATE

BIRD

NOTES

PLACE / DATE

BIRD

NOTES

PLACE / DATE

BIRD

NOTES

PLACE / DATE

BIRD

NOTES

PLACE / DATE

BIRD

NOTES

PLACE / DATE

BIRD

NOTES

PLACE / DATE

BIRD

NOTES

PLACE / DATE

BIRD

NOTES

PLACE / DATE

BIRD

NOTES

PLACE / DATE

BIRD

NOTES

PLACE / DATE

BIRD

NOTES

PLACE / DATE

BIRD

NOTES

PLACE / DATE

BIRD

NOTES

PLACE / DATE

BIRD

NOTES

PLACE / DATE

BIRD

NOTES

Stand-Still Birding

While the energy and momentum of full-speed-ahead birding can mean sighting a large number of species, there's quiet joy in stand-still birding.

Pick a place—forest, field, or marsh. Find a seat that's dry and . . . blend in. Sitting with your back against a tree is especially good. Be still. After perhaps twenty minutes, birds accept you as part of the landscape and go back to their bird business—eating, courting, feeding their young.

If you start with your binoculars held up almost to your eyes, you won't need to make any sudden movement. Slow movement—or no movement—is the key. Perhaps you'll spot a female humming-bird flying back to her secret nest. That's just about the only way you'll ever be able to see one!

Some birds may be curious—or indifferent—and come quite near, allowing you a better look.

This is not about logging species, but about close and contemplative observation. Call it "Zen birding" or "the Big Sit"— you become part of the birds' world.

Bobolink

PLACE / DATE

BIRD

NOTES

PLACE / DATE

BIRD

NOTES

PLACE / DATE

BIRD

NOTES

PLACE / DATE

BIRD

NOTES

PLACE / DATE

BIRD

NOTES

PLACE / DATE

BIRD

NOTES

PLACE / DATE

BIRD

NOTES

PLACE / DATE

BIRD

NOTES

PLACE / DATE

BIRD

NOTES

PLACE / DATE

BIRD

NOTES

PLACE / DATE

BIRD

NOTES

PLACE / DATE

BIRD

NOTES

PLACE / DATE

BIRD

NOTES

PLACE / DATE

BIRD

NOTES

PLACE / DATE

BIRD

NOTES

PLACE / DATE

BIRD

NOTES

PLACE / DATE

BIRD

NOTES

PLACE / DATE

BIRD

NOTES

PLACE / DATE

BIRD

NOTES

PLACE / DATE

BIRD

NOTES

Roadside Birds

Stuck in traffic these days? Inching along with nothing to do? Go birding!

Well-known birding expert David Sibley notes that the territories of all but one regularly occurring landbird species in the Lower Forty-Eight can be seen from a paved surface. That means plenty of birds to view from a car or bus. Of course, birding from the driver's seat can be dangerous, but watchful passengers can find all kinds of avian roadside attractions.

Peregrine Falcons often perch on towers beside bridges, waiting for the unwary Rock Pigeon to fly by. Their smaller cousins, American Kestrels, perch on wires, watching for small rodents or birds or large insects. Football-sized and football-shaped Red-tailed Hawks and other large birds of prey sit on light standards, telephone poles, and trees along the roadside. The highway's center median and mowed shoulders offer these birds a ribbon of open grassland for hunting rabbits, rodents, and small birds. Once a predator discovers a good feeding area, it returns often.

Northern Shrikes and their more southerly cousins, Loggerhead Shrikes, perch beside a grassy open space while they wait for a hapless bird or insect or snake to present itself.

Swallows coast to coast gather and perch on wires in the fall before flying south for the winter. European Starlings gather daily by the hundreds before moving on to their night roost.

In the South, watch for the dashing Scissor-tailed Flycatcher.

There's no mistaking the pink and gray colors and a tail longer than the bird's body.

Many field guides include profile images or silhouettes of the birds. Get to know these, and you'll recognize the bird on the wire at a quick glance.

And what's the one species you shouldn't expect to see in your roadside birding? According to David Sibley, it's the Colima Warbler, a tiny Mexican songster that barely stretches its territory into southern Texas. You'll have to visit Big Bend National Park to see that little bird!

Quail Feather

PLACE / DATE

BIRD

NOTES

PLACE / DATE

BIRD

NOTES

PLACE / DATE

BIRD

NOTES

PLACE / DATE

BIRD

NOTES

PLACE / DATE

BIRD

NOTES

PLACE / DATE

BIRD

NOTES

PLACE / DATE

BIRD

NOTES

PLACE / DATE

BIRD

NOTES

PLACE / DATE

BIRD

NOTES

PLACE / DATE

BIRD

NOTES

PLACE / DATE

BIRD

NOTES

PLACE / DATE

BIRD

NOTES

PLACE / DATE

BIRD

NOTES

PLACE / DATE

BIRD

NOTES

PLACE / DATE

BIRD

NOTES

PLACE / DATE

BIRD

NOTES

PLACE / DATE

BIRD

NOTES

PLACE / DATE

BIRD

NOTES

PLACE / DATE

BIRD

NOTES

PLACE / DATE

BIRD

NOTES

Little Brown Birds

In many parts of the country, the most common backyard birds tend to look the same to the untrained eye. They might be sparrows, wrens, juncos, finches . . . or something altogether different. Learning to tell these unidentified flying objects apart can be really frustrating.

Long ago, birdwatchers came up with whimsical terms to describe them: LBBs, little brown birds, or LBJs, little brown jobs. These small nondescript birds are camouflaged to blend in with dried grass, leaves, and dark underbrush—it's one means of their survival.

But it can be maddening to sort out the "subtle streaking," the "slightly grayer forehead," or the "upright stance"—phrases that bird books use to distinguish the birds.

One solution? Ask a seasoned birder for help. Purchase a basic field guide of your local birds. Ask the birder to put markers on the ten to twelve pages of the birds you are most likely to see in your yard. Then when you spot an LBB, you can flip to the most likely pages and compare the bird on the page to the bird in the yard. You'll soon begin to recognize them.

And the next time you're out for a walk and an unidentified flying object crosses your path, you might surprise yourself by knowing its name.

Anna's Hummingbird

PLACE / DATE

BIRD

NOTES

PLACE / DATE

BIRD

NOTES

PLACE / DATE

BIRD

NOTES

PLACE / DATE

BIRD

NOTES

PLACE / DATE

BIRD

NOTES

PLACE / DATE

BIRD

NOTES

PLACE / DATE

BIRD

NOTES

PLACE / DATE

BIRD

NOTES

PLACE / DATE

BIRD

NOTES

PLACE / DATE

BIRD

NOTES

PLACE / DATE

BIRD

NOTES

PLACE / DATE

BIRD

NOTES

PLACE / DATE

BIRD

NOTES

PLACE / DATE

BIRD

NOTES

PLACE / DATE

BIRD

NOTES

PLACE / DATE

BIRD

NOTES

PLACE / DATE

BIRD

NOTES

PLACE / DATE

BIRD

NOTES

PLACE / DATE

BIRD

NOTES

PLACE / DATE

BIRD

NOTES

Unlikely Places to Go Birding

Location! Location! Location!

Location is just as important in birding as in real estate. But unlike real estate, where the prime location has a panoramic view or great ambience, birding is often best in the most unlikely places.

Sewage treatment plants are great places to look for birds. Watch for gulls, ducks, and the ever-vigilant raptors keeping watch nearby. Swallows find them appealing as night roosts. From northeast Philadelphia to Sweetwater in Tucson, from Arcata Marsh in California to the Wakodahatchee Wetlands in Florida, birds—and birders—turn up in great numbers. Why? The treatment plants offer food, warmth, and cover. Check it out: there may be one near you!

Another place might be your local landfill or dump. From Alaska to southern Texas, dumps are often great places to find birds. The Juneau, Alaska, landfill is famous for its "gathering of gulls," and you used to be able to find lots of ravens there too. And at the other end of the country, the Brownsville, Texas, dump was, for years, the only place in the United States where you could find a Tamaulipas Crow.

Now, for a more sedate birding adventure, consider a visit to a cemetery. Cemeteries are often repositories of native plants, remnants of the native habitats of the nineteenth century. They're magnets for migratory birds, which find food—and cover—in those green oases. They're quiet too.

Birds are where you find 'em.

Tree Swallow

PLACE / DATE

BIRD

NOTES

PLACE / DATE

BIRD

NOTES

PLACE / DATE

BIRD

NOTES

PLACE / DATE

BIRD

NOTES

PLACE / DATE

BIRD

NOTES

PLACE / DATE

BIRD

NOTES

PLACE / DATE

BIRD

NOTES

PLACE / DATE

BIRD

NOTES

PLACE / DATE

BIRD

NOTES

PLACE / DATE

BIRD

NOTES

PLACE / DATE

BIRD

NOTES

PLACE / DATE

BIRD

NOTES

PLACE / DATE

BIRD

NOTES

PLACE / DATE

BIRD

NOTES

PLACE / DATE

BIRD

NOTES

PLACE / DATE

BIRD

NOTES

PLACE / DATE

BIRD

NOTES

PLACE / DATE

BIRD

NOTES

PLACE / DATE

BIRD

NOTES

PLACE / DATE

BIRD

NOTES

Getting to Know Bird Songs and Calls

Sometimes it's impossible to see the bird you hear. Too many leaves, too many pine needles, or maybe you're looking into the sun. Still, you want to know what it is. Well, relax your eyes and let your ears take over!

First, listen for patterns. And think of the sounds as music: Do the notes go up at the end, or down? Are they drawn out? Are they repeated?

You'll find descriptions of birds' songs and calls listed in field guides and online at Cornell Lab's All About Birds. *Peterson Field Guide to Birds of North America* uses terms like "harsh," "pensive," "weak," "bright," "rolling," and "slurred," along with notes about whether the bird sings from the air, from a tree, or on the ground.

Some descriptions are straightforward—like "musical" or "jumbled" or "mechanical." Cornell says the song of the American Robin is "musical" and translates it to "cheerily, cheer up, cheer up, cheerily, cheer up." Further, "the syllables rise and fall in pitch but are delivered at a steady rhythm, with a pause before the bird begins singing again." Listen to a robin, and you'll begin to decipher that.

The translation of bird songs and calls into human language turns up in almost every field guide. Get a good look at a yellowish bird with a black mask, singing in a wetland, and you might hear the "witchety, witchety, witchety" song of a Common Yellowthroat. The White-crowned Sparrow has different dialects across the

United States, but in nearly every one, you can hear some version of "See me, pretty-pretty me."

The song of a Swainson's Thrush is often described as "flutelike" and "upward spiraling." That's quite a contrast to the "plaintively whistled" notes of a Black-capped Chickadee, often found in the same habitat. *Peterson Field Guide* describes the "Quick, three beers" song of the Olive-sided Flycatcher as "a spirited whistle." (A "whistle" is a sound that many humans could imitate, like the songs and calls of that Olive-sided Flycatcher or a Northern Bobwhite or Killdeer.)

And what's the difference between a song and a call? In most species, a song is used primarily during the breeding season to proclaim territory and attract a mate. Calls are generally shorter and simpler. In songbirds, they often signal alarm at a predator or aggression toward a rival, or they maintain contact between members of a pair or flock.

Time to tune up your ears!

Baltimore Oriole Feather

PLACE / DATE

BIRD

NOTES

PLACE / DATE

BIRD

NOTES

PLACE / DATE

BIRD

NOTES

PLACE / DATE

BIRD

NOTES

PLACE / DATE

BIRD

NOTES

PLACE / DATE

BIRD

NOTES

PLACE / DATE

BIRD

NOTES

PLACE / DATE

BIRD

NOTES

PLACE / DATE

BIRD

NOTES

PLACE / DATE

BIRD

NOTES

PLACE / DATE

BIRD

NOTES

PLACE / DATE

BIRD

NOTES

PLACE / DATE

BIRD

NOTES

PLACE / DATE

BIRD

NOTES

PLACE / DATE

BIRD

NOTES

PLACE / DATE

BIRD

NOTES

LIFE LIST

LIFE LIST

LIFE LIST

LIFE LIST

LIFE LIST

LIFE LIST

LIFE LIST

LIFE LIST

LIFE LIST

LIFE LIST

LIFE LIST

LIFE LIST

LIFE LIST

LIFE LIST

LIFE LIST

Printed in China

SASQUATCH BOOKS with colophon is a registered
trademark of Penguin Random House LLC

23 22 21 20 19   9 8 7 6 5 4 3 2 1

Editor: Ellen Blackstone
Production editor: Jill Saginario
Design: Tony Ong
Illustrations: Emily Poole

ISBN: 978-1-63217-284-6

Sasquatch Books
1904 Third Avenue, Suite 710
Seattle, WA 98101
SasquatchBooks.com